How To Outsmart A Narcissistic Ex Husband As A Co-parent.

Protecting Your Child: A Guide to Bouncing Back from a Narcissistic Ex-Lover in a Destructive Marriage – Building Healthy Boundaries and Healing from Emotional Abuse

By Sara C. Blackmon

Copyright/Disclaimer

The information contained in this book is for general instructional purposes only While the author has made every effort to provide accurate and up-to-date information, readers are advised to consult with relevant professionals, such as lawyers, therapists, or counselors, to address their specific concerns and needs related to the topics discussed in this book. The author and publisher shall not be liable for any negative consequences, harm, or legal consequences that may arise from the use or misuse of this book's contents.

While the author has made efforts to protect the privacy and confidentiality of individuals mentioned in the book, characters, and incidents are used for illustrative purposes and any resemblance to actual persons, living or dead, or actual scenario is completely coincidental.

Every effort has been made to respect the intellectual property rights of third parties, and the author and publisher will promptly address any verified claims of copyright infringement regarding materials used in the book, provided the necessary permission was not obtained.

About The Author

Sara C. Blackmon is not just an accomplished psychologist but also a dedicated wife and loving mother. With a profound passion for understanding the complexities of human relationships and emotions, she has spent years delving into the intricacies of psychology to help individuals lead happier and healthier lives. Sara's unique blend of personal and professional experience has equipped her with invaluable insights into navigating the challenging terrain of co-parenting, especially in the presence of a narcissistic ex-lover.

Her commitment to supporting families and empowering individuals to overcome adversity is a driving force behind her work. Through her writing, Sara aspires to share her expertise and guide readers in fostering nurturing, child-centric environments while safeguarding their own well-being in the face of challenging situations. Sara's personal journey, both as a mother and a psychologist, adds depth and authenticity to her words, making her a trusted source of guidance and support for those seeking to thrive in the midst of adversity.

Introduction

Navigating the treacherous waters of co parenting can be a challenging endeavor under the best of circumstances. However, when you add the complexity of dealing with a narcissistic ex-husband into the equation, the journey becomes even more arduous. Coparenting with a narcissist can feel like an uphill battle, where manipulation, conflicts, and power struggles seem to be the order of the day. Yet, amidst this storm, there is hope, and there is a path to not only surviving but thriving as a co parent.

This book is your guide through the labyrinth of coparenting with a narcissistic ex-husband. It is a journey that many have walked before you, each with their unique set of challenges, and each with their own story to tell. I am here to help you navigate this difficult terrain, offering you guidance, support, and strategies to outsmart the narcissist and create a healthier, more stable environment for your child.

In the pages that follow, we will delve deep into the world of narcissism, exploring the traits and behaviors that make coparenting with a narcissistic ex-husband uniquely challenging. We will provide you with practical tools and strategies for effective communication, boundary-setting, and legal recourse. We will emphasize the importance of keeping your child's well-being at the forefront of your co-parenting journey, and we will guide you in building emotional resilience to weather the storms that may come your way.

But this book is not just about surviving. It's about thriving. It's about turning the challenges you face into opportunities for personal growth and empowerment. It's about ensuring that your child's future is filled with love, stability, and the support they need to flourish.

I understand the emotional toll that coparenting with a narcissistic ex-spouse can take, but I also believe in the strength, resilience, and determination of individuals like you who are committed to the well-being of their children. The path ahead may be rocky, but it is not insurmountable. I am here to walk this path with you, to offer a hand of support and guidance as you embark on this journey.

Together, we can outsmart the narcissistic ex-husband and create a brighter future for you and your child.

So, let's begin this journey together, one step at a time, one chapter at a time, with the ultimate goal of thriving as a co parent, despite the challenges that lie ahead.

Understanding Narcissism and Its Impact on Coparenting

Navigating the complexities of coparenting with a narcissistic ex-husband begins with a fundamental understanding of narcissism itself. In this chapter, we delve deep into the world of narcissistic personality traits, providing insight into the nature of narcissism and its impact on co parenting dynamics.

Defining Narcissism

Narcissism is a personality trait characterized by an excessive focus on oneself, an inflated sense of self-importance, and a profound need for admiration and validation. Narcissists often display behaviors that revolve around self-centeredness, grandiosity, and a lack of empathy for others. They see themselves as superior and may demand constant attention and recognition.

Types of Narcissism

Understanding narcissism also involves recognizing that it exists on a spectrum. While some individuals may exhibit narcissistic traits more mildly, others may present as full-blown narcissists. This spectrum includes:

Narcissistic Personality Disorder (NPD): A clinical diagnosis characterized by pervasive patterns of grandiosity, a need for admiration, and a lack of empathy. Coparenting with a diagnosed narcissist often presents significant challenges.

Subclinical Narcissism: This refers to individuals who may not meet the diagnostic criteria for NPD but still display narcissistic traits. Coparents with subclinical narcissism traits can create difficulties as well.

Impact of Narcissism on Coparenting

The presence of narcissistic traits in your ex-husband can profoundly affect the coparenting relationship. Understanding the impact of narcissism is crucial for developing strategies to cope with its challenges:

Manipulation: Narcissists are skilled manipulators. They may use guilt, blame, and other tactics to get their way, making co parenting decisions and communication fraught with power struggles.

Conflict: The constant need for control and admiration can lead to frequent conflicts in coparenting. Understanding the source of these conflicts is the first step in managing and reducing them.

Lack of Empathy: Narcissists often struggle to empathize with others' perspectives, including their children's. This can result in decisions that prioritize their own needs over the well-being of the child.

Inconsistency: Coparenting with a narcissist may involve unpredictable behaviors and decisions. Their need for validation may lead to changes in parenting styles or agreements to gain attention.

Emotional Impact on Children: Children caught in the middle of coparenting with a narcissistic parent may experience emotional and psychological stress. Understanding this impact is crucial for ensuring their well-being.

Effective Coparenting Despite Challenge

Navigating the complex world of coparenting, especially with a narcissistic ex-husband, can be fraught with challenges. However, this chapter is dedicated to equipping you with the knowledge and strategies to effectively coparent, even in the face of adversity.

The Power of Emotional Resilience

Emotional resilience is the cornerstone of effective co parenting. It empowers you to remain steady in the face of adversity and to be a source of stability for your child. Here's how to build and maintain emotional resilience:

Self-Care: Prioritize self-care practices to maintain your emotional well-being. Regular exercise, a balanced diet, adequate sleep, and relaxation techniques can help you manage stress and stay emotionally grounded.

Mindfulness and Meditation: Practicing mindfulness and meditation can help you stay present, reduce anxiety, and better handle difficult situations.

Therapy and Support: Seeking therapy or counseling can provide a safe space to explore your emotions, gain insights, and develop strategies to cope with co parenting challenges.

Support Networks: Lean on your support network of friends, family, and support groups. Talking to others who understand your experiences can provide emotional relief and valuable advice.

Understanding Legal and Mediation Options

In cases of severe conflict or non-compliance with co parenting agreements, it may be necessary to explore legal and mediation options:

Modification of Custody Arrangements: Understand the process for modifying custody arrangements when necessary. Consult with a family law attorney to maneuver the legal aspects.

Mediation: Mediation can be a less adversarial way to resolve disputes and conflicts. A trained mediator can facilitate communication and help you and your ex-spouse reach mutually agreeable solutions.

Alternative Dispute Resolution: Investigate alternative dispute resolution methods, such as collaborative law or arbitration, as less adversarial options to resolve co parenting issues.

Seeking Court Intervention: In cases of severe conflict or safety concerns, consult with an attorney about seeking court intervention. A court order can provide enforceable solutions.

Leveraging Coparenting Tools and Technology

Modern technology offers various tools and apps that can simplify coparenting and minimize direct contact with your ex-spouse:

Co Parenting Apps: Explore co parenting apps designed to facilitate communication, share calendars, and track expenses. These apps can streamline coparenting tasks and reduce the potential for conflict.

Shared Documents: Use shared documents or cloud-based platforms for exchanging important information, such as school schedules, medical records, and visitation details.

Parenting Agreements: Create a detailed parenting plan or agreement that outlines expectations, responsibilities, and routines. This can serve as a reference point and minimize disagreements.

Therapist Involvement: In some cases, consider involving a family therapist or counselor to facilitate communication between you and your ex-spouse, especially when making critical decisions regarding your child's well-being.

The Narcissistic Ex-Husband

A narcissistic ex-husband is an individual who exhibits narcissistic personality traits or, in severe cases, meets the criteria for Narcissistic Personality Disorder (NPD) and is also the former spouse of the individual discussing their experiences. Narcissism, in the context of a personality trait or disorder, is characterized by a range of behaviors and thought patterns that revolve around self-centeredness, grandiosity, a need for admiration and validation, and a lack of empathy for others. These traits often manifest in various ways, making coparenting with a narcissistic ex-husband uniquely challenging.

Key characteristics and behaviors associated with a narcissistic ex-husband may include:

Self-Centeredness: A primary focus on their own needs, desires, and well-being, often at the expense of others, including their children and former spouse.

Grandiosity: An inflated sense of self-importance, viewing themselves as superior to others, and seeking constant admiration and validation.

Manipulation: The use of manipulation tactics to control situations, gain an upper hand, and shape outcomes to their liking. This can include tactics like guilt-tripping, gaslighting, or emotional coercion.

Lack of Empathy: An inability to empathize with the emotions and needs of others, including their children. This can result in a lack of understanding or consideration for the emotional well-being of those involved.

Conflict and Power Struggles: Frequent conflicts and power struggles within the coparenting relationship, often driven by their need for control and admiration.

Inconsistency: Unpredictable behaviors and decision-making, which can create confusion and instability in the coparenting relationship.

Difficulty Sharing Authority: Reluctance to share parenting responsibilities and decision-making, often asserting their authority as the primary or only valid authority.

Projection and Blame: A tendency to project their own shortcomings onto others, often blaming their ex-spouse for problems and conflicts that arise.

Self-Centered Parenting: A focus on their own desires and agenda, sometimes prioritizing their needs above the well-being of their children.

Recognizing Narcissistic Traits and Behaviors

Understanding the nature of narcissistic traits and behaviors is the essential first step in coping with a narcissistic ex-husband and navigating the challenges of coparenting. Here, we delve into the key characteristics and behaviors that are indicative of narcissistic tendencies, enabling you to recognize them when they manifest in your coparenting relationship.

Characteristics of a narcissistic man

Grandiosity

One of the attributes of narcissism is grandiosity. Narcissists possess an inflated sense of self-importance and believe they are exceptional and superior to others. This grandiosity can lead them to expect constant admiration and validation from those around them. Often monopolize conversations
the feeling of been disrespected, mistreated, diminished and enraged when ignored

exploitative relationships: An exploitative relationship is one in which one party takes advantage of the other, often for their own benefit, while disregarding the well-being, rights, or needs of the exploited individual.

Lack of Empathy

Empathy, narcissists often lack the capacity to understand and share the feelings of others. They have difficulty recognizing and empathizing with the emotional needs and experiences of their children and former spouses. This lack of empathy can be particularly pronounced in high-conflict co parenting situations.

Manipulation

Narcissists are skilled manipulators. They use various tactics to control situations, gain an upper hand, and shape outcomes in their favor. Common manipulation tactics in coparenting may include guilt-tripping, gaslighting (distorting facts and reality), or emotional coercion.

Projection and Blame

Narcissists have a tendency to project their own shortcomings and insecurities onto others, often blaming them for the issues and conflicts that arise. This projection and blame-shifting can complicate co parenting interactions.

Conflict and Power Struggles

The need for control and admiration can lead to frequent conflicts and power struggles in co parenting relationships with narcissists. These struggles may arise from their unwillingness to compromise or share authority.

Inconsistency

Narcissists can be unpredictable in their behaviors and decision-making. They may change their stance or approach based on their immediate need for validation or admiration. This inconsistency can create confusion and instability in co parenting arrangements.

Coping with Manipulation and Emotional Challenges

Coparenting with a narcissistic ex-husband often involves contending with manipulation and emotional challenges that can test your patience, resilience, and emotional well-being. Here, we will explore practical strategies to cope with the manipulative behaviors of a narcissist and navigate the emotional rollercoaster that can accompany such interactions.

Recognizing Manipulation

Narcissists are adept at manipulation, and it is crucial to recognize the tactics they may employ in coparenting:

Guilt-Tripping: Narcissists may use guilt to pressure you into decisions or actions that align with their desires, often making you question your choices.

Gaslighting: Gaslighting involves distorting facts and reality to make you doubt your own perceptions and sanity, which can be especially disorienting in a coparenting relationship.

Triangulation: The narcissist may involve others, such as family members or friends, to manipulate the situation or gain support for their perspective.

Silent Treatment: Silence can be a form of manipulation, where the narcissist withholds communication or cooperation as a means to control or punish you.

Strategies to Cope with Manipulation

Maintain Clarity: Keep a record of communications and agreements to counter gaslighting and manipulation attempts. Having written documentation can provide clarity and protect your interests.

Set Boundaries: Clearly define your boundaries and communicate them to your ex-spouse. Establishing and maintaining boundaries can help deter manipulative behaviors.

Stay Emotionally Detached: Practice emotional detachment by learning to recognize when manipulation is occurring. Avoid reacting emotionally and instead respond calmly and rationally.

Seek Support: Share your experiences with a trusted friend, therapist, or support group. Talking to someone who understands your challenges can provide emotional relief.

Navigating Emotional Challenges

The emotional toll of co-parenting with a narcissist can be profound. It's important to recognize and address these challenges:

Frustration and Anger: Dealing with manipulation and conflict can lead to frustration and anger. It's essential to find healthy ways to release these emotions, such as through exercise or therapy.

Stress and Anxiety: Co Parenting can be a source of constant stress and anxiety. Implement stress management techniques, like mindfulness or deep breathing exercises, to regain your composure.

Guilt and Self-Doubt: Narcissists often project blame onto others. Recognize that their actions are not a reflection of your worth. Combat feelings of guilt and self-doubt with self-compassion.

Loneliness and Isolation: Co Parenting difficulties can make you feel isolated. Reach out to a support network, and consider joining local or online co parenting support groups.

Strategies for Successful Co Parenting

Coparenting with a narcissistic ex-husband can be an uphill battle, but it's not an insurmountable one. This chapter is dedicated to providing you with practical strategies and guidance to navigate the complexities of co parenting effectively, all while keeping your child's best interests at heart.

Communication Techniques for High-Conflict Situations

Effective communication is the cornerstone of any successful co parenting relationship. When dealing with a high-conflict co parent, it becomes even more critical to employ specific communication techniques to navigate the complexities and reduce tensions. In this chapter, we will explore practical strategies and approaches that can help you communicate more effectively in high-conflict situations with a narcissistic ex-husband.

Keep It Brief and Neutral

In high-conflict co parenting, it's crucial to keep your communication brief and neutral. Avoid engaging in emotional language or personal attacks. Stick to the facts, focusing on the matter at hand, and avoid veering off into unrelated topics or grievances.

Use Written Communication

Written communication can be highly effective in high-conflict co parenting situations. Consider using email, text messages, or dedicated co parenting apps to communicate. Written communication leaves a clear record and minimizes the potential for misunderstandings or manipulation.

Avoid Jargon: Steer clear of psychological or legal jargon that can be used against you. Use straightforward, plain language to minimize confusion and conflict. Clear and simple communication is often the most effective.

Parallel Parenting: In cases of extreme conflict, parallel parenting can be a viable approach. Parallel parenting involves minimizing direct contact and communication with your ex-spouse. Each parent manages their responsibilities separately, reducing the potential for conflict. This approach can provide a sense of separation while still ensuring the child's well-being.

Document Agreements and Violations: Keeping a record of all agreements and violations can be a powerful tool in high-conflict co parenting. Document all discussions, decisions, and agreements in writing. If your ex-husband violates these agreements, have a record to reference. Documenting violations can be helpful if legal intervention becomes necessary.

Practice Emotional Detachment: In high-conflict situations, emotional detachment is essential. Recognize when your ex-husband's communication is intended to provoke an emotional reaction. Instead of reacting emotionally, respond calmly and rationally. This helps you maintain control of the situation and reduces the opportunity for escalating conflicts.

Seek Support: Do not hesitate to reach out for support when dealing with high-conflict co parenting. Share your experiences and frustrations with a trusted friend, family member, therapist, or a support group. Talking to someone who understands your challenges can provide emotional relief and valuable insights.

Establish Clear Boundaries: Setting and maintaining boundaries is crucial when dealing with a high-conflict co parent. Clearly define your boundaries and expectations, and communicate them to your ex-spouse. Establishing and maintaining boundaries can deter manipulative behaviors and minimize conflict.

Utilize Co Parenting Apps: Consider using co parenting apps specifically designed to facilitate communication between coparents. These apps often include features like shared calendars, expense tracking, and messaging, streamlining coparenting tasks and minimizing direct contact.

Establishing and Maintaining Boundaries

Boundaries are a crucial component of any healthy relationship, especially when dealing with a high-conflict co parenting situation involving a narcissistic ex-husband. Boundaries are not a sign of weakness but an indication of self-respect and a commitment to maintaining a healthy co parenting relationship. By establishing and consistently maintaining clear boundaries, you create a more stable and respectful environment for you and your child, even in the face of a narcissistic ex-husband. Here we will focus on the importance of establishing and maintaining clear boundaries to create a more stable and respectful coparenting dynamic.

The Significance of Boundaries in Coparenting

In the context of coparenting, boundaries serve several essential purposes:

Conflict Prevention: Clearly defined boundaries can prevent misunderstandings and conflicts. They provide guidelines for behavior and interaction, reducing the potential for clashes.

Emotional Protection: Boundaries protect your emotional well-being. They establish limits that help prevent emotional manipulation and abuse from your ex-spouse.

Respect: Boundaries convey the expectation of respect. By setting and enforcing boundaries, you demand respect for your rights, feelings, and personal space.

Safety: In some cases, boundaries can ensure physical safety and the well-being of you and your child.

Establishing Clear Boundaries

Identify Your Needs: Reflect on your personal needs and priorities in the coparenting relationship. Determine what behaviors and interactions are acceptable and which cross the line.

Communicate Your Boundaries: Clearly and assertively communicate your boundaries to your ex-husband. Use "I" statements to express your needs and feelings without blaming or accusing.

Be Specific: When setting boundaries, be specific about what is and isn't acceptable. For example, if you want communication to occur only through email or a co parenting app, make that explicit.

Prioritize Your Child: Ensure that your boundaries are aligned with your child's best interests. This helps emphasize that the boundaries are not about personal preferences but about creating a healthy environment for your child.

Consistency is Key: Consistency in enforcing boundaries is crucial. Your ex-husband should know that your boundaries are non-negotiable and will be consistently upheld.

Seek Professional Guidance: In particularly challenging situations, it can be beneficial to involve a therapist, mediator, or counselor to facilitate boundary discussions. Their expertise can help both parties understand and respect each other's boundaries.

Maintaining Boundaries in High-Conflict Co Parenting

Stay Firm: Expect resistance when you establish or maintain boundaries, especially in high-conflict situations. Stay firm in your commitment to uphold your boundaries.

Avoid Engagement: In cases where your ex-husband attempts to violate boundaries, do not engage in conflict or emotional confrontations. Stick to your established boundaries calmly and confidently.

Seek Legal Intervention When Necessary: If your ex-spouse constantly violates your boundaries and poses a threat to your safety or the child's well-being, consult with an attorney about seeking legal intervention or court orders to enforce boundaries.

Self-Care: Prioritize self-care practices to maintain your emotional well-being and resilience. Coping with a high-conflict co parent can be emotionally draining, and self-care is essential for maintaining your strength.

Putting Your Child First

In the intricate dance of coparenting with a narcissistic ex-husband, it can be easy to become ensnared in conflicts, manipulation, and personal grievances. However, the ultimate priority in this journey is the well-being and welfare of your child. Putting your child first in coparenting with a narcissistic ex-husband may require great patience and resilience. However, it is an investment in their well-being and emotional development. Your child's future and happiness are worth the effort. In this chapter, we will explore the principles and strategies for consistently putting your child first, even in high-conflict co parenting situations.

Child-Centered Decision-Making

The foundation of a successful co parenting relationship lies in making decisions based on the best interests of your child. This approach requires:

Objective Evaluation: Prioritize your child's physical and emotional needs above all else.

When making decisions, evaluate how they will impact your child's overall well-being, safety, and development.

Open Communication: Practicalize open and honest communication with your child. Make them feel safe discussing their feelings, concerns, and experiences related to the co parenting situation.

Consistency and Routine: Strive to maintain consistent routines and schedules between households. Children thrive on predictability and stability, so aligning routines with your ex-spouse can provide that necessary sense of security.

Flexibility and Compromise: While it can be challenging to cooperate with a narcissistic ex-husband, make efforts to find common ground. Compromise when it benefits your child, even if it means tolerating certain inconveniences.

Cooperation Over Conflict

Minimizing conflict and prioritizing cooperation can significantly benefit your child. Here's how to do that:

Focus on Shared Goals: Instead of dwelling on past conflicts or grievances, concentrate on shared goals for your child's well-being, safety, and happiness.

Effective Communication: Employ the communication techniques discussed in the previous chapter, such as keeping communication brief, neutral, and in writing, to reduce the potential for conflict.

Pick Your Battles: Not every issue requires a confrontation. Determine which matters are most critical for your child's well-being and focus your energy on those.

Mediation and Therapy: In some cases, involve a mediator or therapist to facilitate communication between you and your ex-spouse. Professional guidance can often bridge gaps and help both parties see the bigger picture.

Open Dialogue with Your Child

Encourage your child to express their thoughts, feelings, and concerns about the co-parenting situation. By fostering open dialogue, you can help them:

Feel Heard: Listening to your child validates their experiences and emotions, reinforcing their sense of self-worth.

Manage Emotions: Open communication allows your child to discuss any distress they may be experiencing due to the co-parenting situation, giving them an outlet for their emotions.

Provide Reassurance: Reassure your child that they are loved and supported by both parents, even if the circumstances are challenging.

Consistent Parenting Styles

Strive for consistency in parenting styles between households. Align on important principles, rules, and consequences. When your child experiences a consistent approach to parenting, it reduces confusion and anxiety.

Keeping Conflict Away from Your Child

Shield your child from the brunt of co parenting conflicts by:

Selective Sharing: Be mindful of the information you share with your child. Avoid discussing adult matters, conflicts, or personal grievances with them.

Modeling Healthy Behavior: Demonstrate healthy conflict resolution and communication strategies in front of your child. They learn by example, and your behavior can set a positive model.

Safe Space: Create a safe and open space for your child to discuss their feelings and concerns without judgment.

Navigating Coparenting with a Child-Centered Approach

In the tumultuous waters of coparenting with a narcissistic ex-husband, keeping your child at the heart of your decisions is paramount. A child-centered approach not only ensures your child's well-being but also serves as a compass to navigate the complexities of high-conflict co parenting. A child-centered approach is a guiding light in high-conflict co parenting situations. It ensures that your child's well-being remains at the forefront of all decisions and interactions. By consistently putting your child first, you create an environment in which they can thrive and feel secure despite the challenges they may face. Here, we delve into practical strategies for maintaining a child-centered approach.

The Core Principles of a Child-Centered Approach

Prioritizing Your Child's Needs: Make your child's well-being the primary focus of all co parenting decisions. Consider their physical, emotional, and developmental needs when making choices.

Open and Honest Communication: Maintain an environment in which your child feels comfortable sharing their thoughts, concerns, and experiences. Encourage them to express their feelings about the co-parenting situation.

Emotional Support: Reassure your child that they are loved and supported by both parents. Create a safe space for them to discuss any emotions or challenges they may be facing.

Consistency and Stability: Strive to provide your child with consistent routines and rules between households. Predictability and stability are essential for their well-being.

Practical Strategies for a Child-Centered Approach

Create a Joint Parenting Plan: Collaborate with your ex-spouse to create a parenting plan that outlines the roles and responsibilities of each parent. A jointly agreed-upon plan ensures that both parents are committed to putting the child's needs first.

Focus on Shared Values: While you and your ex-husband may have differences, identify shared values and principles related to parenting. Emphasize these shared beliefs to maintain consistency in your child's upbringing.

Shared Decision-Making: Involve your child in age-appropriate decision-making processes. When children have a say in decisions that affect their lives, they may feel a sense of empowerment and investment in the outcome.

Avoid Parentification: Be cautious not to place adult responsibilities or emotional burdens on your child. It's essential for them to maintain their role as a child, rather than becoming a mediator or caregiver for you or your ex-spouse.

Embrace Flexibility: A child-centered approach may require flexibility. Be willing to adapt to changes and unexpected situations that arise in the coparenting relationship to best meet your child's needs.

Seek Professional Guidance: If your child is struggling with the co-parenting situation, consider involving a child therapist or counselor. Professional guidance can provide support and coping strategies for your child during challenging times.

Emphasize Quality Time: Prioritize quality time with your child, both individually and as a family. Engage in activities that promote bonding and create positive memories.

Refrain from Negative Talk: Avoid speaking negatively about your ex-husband in front of your child. Such behavior can be emotionally damaging and detrimental to their perception of the other parent.

Stay Informed: Keep abreast of your child's school, social, and extracurricular activities. Being informed allows you to provide appropriate support and encouragement.

Celebrate Milestones Together: When possible, celebrate significant milestones and events in your child's life together as a family, even if you do so separately. This demonstrates unity in your commitment to your child's happiness and achievements.

Fostering a Stable and Supportive Environment

In the challenging landscape of coparenting with a narcissistic ex-husband, creating a stable and supportive environment for your child is paramount. A nurturing atmosphere can help them thrive, even in the face of conflicts and high-conflict dynamics.Fostering a stable and supportive environment in high-conflict co parenting situations can be challenging, but it is a gift you can give your child. By consistently creating a nurturing atmosphere and addressing their emotional needs, you help them grow and develop resilience in the face of adversity. Here, we will explore practical strategies for establishing and maintaining a stable and supportive environment.

The Importance of a Stable and Supportive Environment

Emotional Well-being: A stable and supportive environment helps your child develop a sense of emotional security and stability. This can buffer the impact of coparenting conflicts and the behavior of a narcissistic ex-husband.

Healthy Development: Children in stable environments tend to have healthier emotional, social, and cognitive development. They are more likely to achieve their potential and overcome challenges.

Resilience: A supportive environment equips your child with the tools to cope with adversity and stress. It fosters resilience, enabling them to navigate the ups and downs of life.

Positive Coping Mechanisms: In a stable environment, children learn positive coping mechanisms that can serve them well throughout their lives. They observe and emulate healthy ways of managing challenges.

Practical Strategies for a Stable and Supportive Environment

Consistent Routines: Maintain consistent daily routines, especially when it comes to sleep, mealtimes, and homework. Consistency provides a sense of security.

Safe Space: Ensure that your child feels safe and supported in both households. Encourage them to express their feelings and concerns without fear of judgment or reprisal.

Quality Time: Dedicate quality time for one-on-one interactions with your child. Engage in activities that promote bonding, such as reading, playing games, or taking walks together.

Maintain Boundaries: Keep boundaries consistent and clear. Boundaries help your child understand expectations and provide a sense of safety.

Cooperate with Your Ex-Spouse: Even in a high-conflict situation, strive to cooperate with your ex-husband when it comes to parenting decisions and routines. Present a united front in the best interests of your child.

Emphasize Positive Communication: Encourage open, positive, and constructive communication. Model this behavior for your child, demonstrating how conflicts can be resolved without aggression or hostility.

Therapeutic Support: If your child is struggling with the co-parenting situation, consider involving a child therapist or counselor. Professional guidance can provide valuable coping strategies and support.

Peer Relationships: Foster and support your child's peer relationships and friendships. Encourage them to socialize and spend time with friends outside of the family environment.

Celebrate Achievements: Acknowledge and celebrate your child's achievements and milestones, no matter how small. This reinforces their self-esteem and self-worth.

Emotional Intelligence: Promote the development of emotional intelligence in your child. Encourage them to identify and express their emotions in healthy ways.

Healthy Role Models: Introduce your child to positive role models who can provide additional support and guidance outside of the immediate family.

Self-Care: Prioritize self-care for yourself as a parent. Your own well-being is essential for creating a stable and supportive environment for your child.

Building Emotional Resilience

In the realm of coparenting with a narcissistic ex-husband, emotional resilience is your armor. It's the inner strength that empowers you to navigate the challenges, stay focused on your child's well-being, and maintain your own mental and emotional health. Building emotional resilience is an ongoing journey, and it may take time and effort. However, it is a powerful tool for maintaining your mental and emotional health while navigating the complexities of coparenting with a narcissistic ex-husband. In this chapter, we explore strategies to build and sustain emotional resilience in the face of high-conflict co parenting.

Understanding Emotional Resilience

Emotional resilience is the ability to adapt and bounce back from adversity, stress, and significant life challenges. It's about facing difficult situations with the capacity to manage emotions, maintain perspective, and emerge stronger. In the context of coparenting with a narcissistic ex-husband, emotional resilience is critical for several reasons:

Conflict Management: High-conflict situations can take a toll on your emotional well-being. Resilience helps you manage and reduce the emotional impact of conflicts.

Stress Reduction: Coparenting with a narcissistic ex-husband can be highly stressful. Resilience equips you with the tools to handle stress and prevent it from overwhelming you.

Emotional Health: Resilience contributes to your overall emotional health and stability. It helps you maintain a positive outlook and emotional balance.

Positive Co Parenting: Building resilience enables you to approach co parenting challenges with a solutions-focused mindset, benefiting your child and the overall coparenting relationship.

Strategies for Building Emotional Resilience

Self-Care: Prioritize self-care activities that support your mental and emotional well-being. This may include exercise, relaxation techniques, hobbies, or any activities that bring you joy and relaxation.

Seek Support: Lean on your support network, which may include friends, family, or a therapist. Sharing your experiences and feelings with trusted persons can provide emotional relief.

Mindfulness and Meditation: Practice mindfulness and meditation techniques to stay grounded and focused on the present moment. These practices can help you manage stress and reduce anxiety.

Positive Self-Talk: Stand against negative self-talk and replace it with positive affirmations. Remind yourself of your strengths and resilience.

Set Realistic Expectations: Avoid setting unrealistic expectations for yourself in high-conflict co parenting. Recognize that there will be challenges, and it's okay to seek help when needed.

Maintain Boundaries: Uphold your boundaries to protect your emotional well-being. Don't allow your ex-spouse's behavior to invade your personal space.

Adaptability: Cultivate adaptability and the ability to pivot in response to changing circumstances. Being open to alternative solutions can reduce emotional strain.

Problem-Solving Skills: Enhance your problem-solving skills, which will allow you to address co parenting challenges with a solutions-focused mindset.

Positive Coping Mechanisms: Develop healthy coping mechanisms to manage stress and emotions. This may include journaling, creative outlets, or physical activities.

Focus on Self-Growth: See challenging situations as opportunities for personal growth. This mindset shift can enhance your resilience.

Accept What You Can't Change: Recognize that there are elements of the coparenting relationship that you cannot control. Focus on what you can influence and accept the rest.

Stay Child-Centered: Continuously remind yourself that your child's well-being is the ultimate goal. This perspective can provide motivation and strength.

Self-Care for Coparents: Managing Stress and Prioritizing Well-Being

In the challenging terrain of coparenting with a narcissistic ex-husband, self-care isn't a luxury; it's a necessity. Managing stress and prioritizing your well-being is essential for your emotional and mental health, and it also benefits your child. Remember that self-care is an ongoing practice, not a one-time solution. Make it a consistent part of your life to manage stress effectively and maintain your well-being. By taking care of yourself, you can approach co-parenting challenges with greater strength and resilience, benefiting both you and your child. Here, we will explore practical strategies for self-care to help you cope with the demands of coparenting.

The Importance of Self-Care

Self-care involves the deliberate and consistent practice of activities that promote your physical, emotional, and mental well-being. It is crucial for several reasons:

Stress Management: Coparenting with a narcissistic ex-husband can be highly stressful. Self-care provides essential tools to manage stress effectively.

Emotional Resilience: Self-care helps build emotional resilience, allowing you to bounce back from challenges and maintain a positive outlook.

Health and Well-Being: Prioritizing self-care contributes to your overall health and well-being, both physically and mentally.

Positive Co Parenting: When you take care of yourself, you are better equipped to engage in positive and constructive co parenting interactions, benefiting your child.

Practical Self-Care Strategies for Coparents

Establish Routine: Create a daily and weekly routine that incorporates self-care activities. This routine can provide a sense of predictability and structure.

Physical Health: Prioritize regular exercise, a balanced diet, and adequate sleep. Physical health is jointly linked to mental and emotional well-being.

Relaxation Techniques: Explore relaxation techniques such as meditation, deep breathing, or progressive muscle relaxation to manage stress.

Seek Support: Lean on your support network. Share your experiences and feelings with friends, family, or a therapist to release emotional tension.

Set Boundaries: Maintain boundaries to protect your personal space and emotional health. Don't allow your ex-spouse's behavior to encroach on your well-being.

Quality Time: Dedicate quality time to activities you enjoy, whether it's reading, hobbies, or socializing with friends. These moments of joy and relaxation are necessary,

Connect with Your Child: Spend one-on-one time with your child, engaging in activities they love. This not only nurtures your relationship but also provides you both with emotional support.

Creative Outlets: Explore creative outlets that allow you to express your emotions and reduce stress. This may include writing, art, music, or any activity that brings you joy.

Positivity and Gratitude: Practice positivity and gratitude by keeping a journal or simply reflecting on the things you're grateful for. This mindset shift can enhance your well-being.

Adopt a Healthy Work-Life Balance: Ensure a balance between your professional life and your responsibilities as a co parent. Overextending yourself can lead to burnout.

Personal Development: Pursue personal development by taking up new interests or learning opportunities. Expanding your horizons can boost self-esteem and resilience.

Say No When Necessary: Don't hesitate to say no to additional commitments when your plate is already full. Your well-being and that of your child should be a top priority.

Professional Help: In cases of severe stress or emotional strain, consider seeking professional help, such as therapy or counseling, to support your mental health.

Seeking Support: Therapy, Support Groups, and Trusted Allies

In the complex world of coparenting with a narcissistic ex-husband, seeking support is not a sign of weakness but a sign of wisdom. Having a support system in place can provide the emotional, mental, and practical assistance you need to navigate the challenges. Seeking support is a vital component of successfully navigating co parenting challenges. Whether through therapy, support groups, or trusted allies, your support system can offer guidance, validation, and relief as you manage the complexities of coparenting with a narcissistic ex-husband. Here, we explore various avenues of support, including therapy, support groups, and trusted allies.

Co-Workers or Colleagues: In some cases, colleagues or coworkers may serve as allies and sources of support, especially if they have faced similar challenges.

Legal and Mediation Professionals: Legal professionals and mediators can offer guidance on navigating the legal aspects of coparenting, providing valuable insights into your rights and responsibilities.

Religious or Spiritual Communities: If you are part of a religious or spiritual community, you may find emotional and practical support within your faith-based network.

Online Forums and Communities: There are online communities and forums dedicated to co parenting and dealing with high-conflict ex-spouses. Engaging in these communities can provide access to a wealth of advice and shared experiences.

Tips for Seeking Support

Identify Your Needs: Determine what kind of support you require, whether it's emotional, practical, or informational.

Set Realistic Expectations: Understand that not all individuals or support avenues will provide the same level of help. Accept different types of support.

Confidentiality: Ensure that your chosen support system provides a safe and confidential space for discussing your concerns.

Consistency: Maintain consistent contact with your support network. Regular communication can help you build and strengthen relationships.

Professional Help: If your situation is particularly challenging or stressful, consider seeking professional guidance from a therapist or counselor.

Support for Your Child: Remember to involve your child in supportive networks as well, such as child therapy or support groups designed to help them cope with the challenges of coparenting.

Legal and Mediation Options

In the intricate landscape of coparenting with a narcissistic ex-husband, legal and mediation options can serve as invaluable tools for resolving disputes, establishing boundaries, and ensuring your child's well-being. Legal and mediation options provide structured mechanisms for addressing and resolving conflicts in coparenting with a narcissistic ex-husband. When used effectively, they can help establish boundaries, protect your child's well-being, and create a more stable coparenting environment. In this chapter, we explore the various legal and mediation avenues available to cope with high-conflict co parenting situations.

When to Consider Legal and Mediation Options

High-Conflict Disputes: If you frequently engage in disputes or conflicts with your ex-husband, especially those related to parenting decisions or visitation arrangements, it may be time to consider legal intervention.

Violation of Court Orders: If your ex-husband constantly violates court-ordered agreements or parenting plans, it is a clear signal to explore legal remedies.

Safety Concerns: If you have concerns about your child's safety or well-being when in your ex-husband's care, it's essential to address these concerns through legal means.

Complex Custody Arrangements: In cases involving complex custody arrangements or international co parenting, mediation and legal assistance can be particularly beneficial.

Legal Options for Coparents

Modification of Court Orders: If circumstances change, such as a significant shift in your ex-husband's behavior or your child's needs, you can seek a modification of court orders to reflect the new situation.

Enforcement of Court Orders: If your ex-husband constantly violates court orders, you can request enforcement through legal means. This may involve penalties for non-compliance.

Child Custody Evaluation: In high-conflict cases, a child custody evaluation by a court-appointed professional may be ordered. This evaluation assesses the child's best interests and can inform custody decisions.

Restraining Orders: If you have concerns about your safety or the safety of your child due to harassment or threats, you can seek a restraining order to protect against contact.

Parental Alienation Claims: In cases of parental alienation, where one parent undermines the child's relationship with the other parent, legal action may be taken to address this issue.

Mediation Options for Coparents

Parenting Mediation: Parenting mediation involves a neutral third party who helps co parents work together to resolve conflicts and make decisions about parenting issues.

Child-Focused Mediation: In child-focused mediation, the primary focus is on the child's best interests. The mediator helps co parents make decisions that benefit the child.

Online Mediation: Online mediation allows parents to engage in mediation sessions remotely, which can be especially useful when dealing with international co parenting situations.

Therapeutic Mediation: In cases where emotional issues or mental health concerns are at play, therapeutic mediation involves a mental health professional who guides co parents toward healthier interactions.

Tips for Navigating Legal and Mediation Options

Consult an Attorney: Seek legal counsel when considering legal options. An attorney can provide advice and guidance tailored to your specific situation.

Document Violations: Maintain detailed records of any violations of court orders or problematic interactions with your ex-husband. These records can be valuable in legal proceedings.

Choose a Skilled Mediator: When selecting a mediator, opt for someone experienced in coparenting and high-conflict dynamics. A skilled mediator can facilitate more productive discussions.

Keep the Child's Best Interests in Mind: Regardless of the legal or mediation route you choose, always prioritize your child's best interests. Your decisions and actions should reflect their welfare.

Maintain Open Communication: Despite the conflict, maintain open communication with your ex-husband during legal proceedings or mediation. This can facilitate problem-solving and resolution.

Understanding Legal Recourse: Modifying Custody Arrangements

In the intricate journey of coparenting with a narcissistic ex-husband, the need for modifying custody arrangements can arise due to changing circumstances, safety concerns, or the best interests of your child. Modifying custody arrangements is a complex legal process, and the best interests of your child should be the guiding principle. When faced with changing circumstances or safety concerns, it's crucial to consider this legal recourse to ensure that your child's welfare is safeguarded in the coparenting dynamic. Here, we will delve into the intricacies of understanding legal recourse for modifying custody arrangements.

When to Consider Modification

Modifying custody arrangements is an option to consider when:
Changing Circumstances: Significant changes in your ex-husband's behavior, living situation, or your child's needs require adjustments to the existing custody arrangement.

Safety Concerns: If you have concerns about your child's safety when in your ex-husband's care, modification may be necessary to ensure their well-being.

Consistent Violations: When your ex-husband constantly violates court-ordered agreements, it's a clear sign that the custody arrangement is not working as intended.

Child's Best Interests: If the current custody arrangement no longer serves the best interests of your child, a modification may be required to better address their needs.

Legal Recourse for Modification

Consult an Attorney: Seek legal counsel to understand the process of modifying custody arrangements in your jurisdiction. An attorney can provide guidance tailored to your specific situation.

Petition the Court: To initiate the modification process, you will need to file a formal request with the court. This is typically done by submitting a petition for modification.

Establish a Substantial Change: The court will typically require evidence of a substantial change in circumstances that justifies the modification. This could include evidence of your ex-husband's behavior, living conditions, or your child's needs.

Child Custody Evaluation: In high-conflict cases, the court may order a child custody evaluation, conducted by a court-appointed professional. This evaluation assesses the child's best interests and informs custody decisions.

Modification Hearing: Once the petition is filed, the court will schedule a modification hearing where both parties present their cases. It's essential to be prepared and present evidence to support your request for modification.

Consider Mediation: In some cases, mediation may be a suitable alternative to litigation. If both you and your ex-husband are willing to engage in productive discussions, a mediated agreement can be submitted to the court.

Tips for Modifying Custody Arrangements

Prioritize Your Child's Well-Being: Ensure that any request for modification is grounded in your child's best interests. The court's foremost concern is the welfare of the child.

Document Violations: Maintain meticulous records of any violations of court orders, disputes, or issues that necessitate a modification. These records can be crucial in court.

Consult with Experts: Consider seeking expert advice. A child custody evaluator, therapist, or counselor may provide valuable insights and evidence to support your case.

Maintain Open Communication: Despite the conflict, maintain open and constructive communication with your ex-husband, especially when discussing potential modifications.

Prepare for the Hearing: Be thoroughly prepared for the modification hearing. Present your case clearly and provide any necessary evidence to support your request.

Mediation and Alternative Dispute Resolution Methods

In the challenging journey of coparenting with a narcissistic ex-husband, mediation and alternative dispute resolution (ADR) methods offer avenues for resolving conflicts, improving communication, and fostering cooperative coparenting. Mediation and ADR offer effective means to navigate the challenges of coparenting with a narcissistic ex-husband. They promote conflict resolution, cooperative communication, and empower co parents to actively participate in making decisions for the benefit of their child. Here we explore the benefits and strategies of mediation and ADR in high-conflict co parenting situations.

The Role of Mediation and ADR in Coparenting

Conflict Resolution: Mediation and ADR provide structured processes for resolving conflicts and disputes between co parents in a neutral and non-adversarial environment.

Cooperative Communication: These methods encourage productive communication between coparents, helping them work together to make decisions in the best interests of their child.

Efficiency: Mediation and ADR can be more efficient than legal proceedings, offering quicker resolutions while reducing the emotional and financial costs of litigation.

Empowerment: Coparents have the opportunity to actively participate in finding solutions to their issues, which can empower them and provide a sense of ownership over the decisions.

Mediation Strategies for Coparents

Select an Experienced Mediator: Choose a mediator with experience in family law and high-conflict situations. They should be well-versed in the complexities of coparenting dynamics.

Establish Ground Rules: At the outset, agree on ground rules for the mediation process. These may include guidelines for respectful communication and adhering to the agenda.

Identify Key Issues: Prioritize the most pressing issues to address during mediation. Focus on areas where resolution is most needed for the well-being of your child.

Open Communication: Approach mediation with an open and cooperative mindset. Listen actively to your ex-husband's concerns and perspectives, and communicate your own.

Seek Common Ground: Recognise areas of agreement and build upon them. Finding common ground can serve as a foundation for reaching consensus on other issues.

Keep the Child's Best Interests in Mind: At all times, prioritize the best interests of your child. Use this as a guiding principle in the decision-making process.

Alternative Dispute Resolution Methods

Collaborative Law: In collaborative law, both coparents, along with their attorneys, commit to resolving disputes cooperatively without litigation. This process often involves multidisciplinary teams, including therapists and financial experts.

Arbitration: In arbitration, a neutral third party acts as a decision-maker, similar to a judge. Both parents present their case, and the arbitrator makes a binding decision.

Online Dispute Resolution: Technology can facilitate online mediation and ADR, making it accessible and convenient, especially in international or long-distance co-parenting situations.

Tips for Successful Mediation and ADR

Be Prepared: Prior to mediation, prepare any necessary documents and evidence to support your position.

Control Emotions: Maintain emotional control during the process.Concentrate on the issues at hand and prevent personal attacks.

Be Flexible: Be open to compromise and alternative solutions. Flexibility can lead to more efficient problem-solving.

Implement Agreements: Once an agreement is reached, ensure it is implemented consistently and adhered to by both coparents.

Co-Parenting Tools and Technology

In the modern age of coparenting, technology can be a valuable ally in managing schedules, facilitating communication, and streamlining the coparenting process. Co-parenting tools and technology can significantly improve communication and organization in your coparenting relationship, especially in high-conflict situations. They offer a structured and secure means of managing schedules, documenting important information, and fostering a child-centric approach to coparenting.This chapter explores co-parenting tools and technology to enhance collaboration and organization in your coparenting relationship.

Benefits of Co-Parenting Tools and Technology

Efficient Communication: Technology provides efficient means for communication, reducing the need for direct, potentially confrontational interactions.

Organized Scheduling: Co-parenting apps and tools allow you to create and manage schedules, ensuring that both parents are on the same page regarding visitation, school events, and other commitments.

Documentation: Tools provide a platform for documenting important information, including medical records, school reports, and financial transactions, which can be valuable in legal proceedings if necessary.

Reduction of Miscommunication: Clear, written communication can reduce misunderstandings and miscommunication, which often occur in high-conflict co parenting situations.

Child-Centric Focus: Many co-parenting tools are designed with the child's best interests in mind, fostering a more child-centric approach to co parenting.

Co-Parenting Tools and Technology Options

Co-Parenting Apps: Several apps, such as OurFamilyWizard, Coparently, and TalkingParents, offer features for communication, scheduling, and expense tracking. These apps allow both co parents to access and update information.

Shared Online Calendars: Platforms like Google Calendar or Apple Calendar can be used to create shared calendars for scheduling visitation, school events, and extracurricular activities.

Messaging Apps: Secure messaging apps like WhatsApp or Signal can facilitate direct communication without the need for personal phone numbers.

Email Platforms: Encrypted email services and platforms can provide a secure channel for written communication.

Document Sharing Services: Google Drive, Dropbox, or Microsoft OneDrive enable the sharing of important documents, such as medical records, report cards, and financial documents.

Tips for Using Co-Parenting Tools and Technology

Choose the Right Tool: Select a tool or technology that aligns with your specific needs and the level of cooperation between you and your ex-husband.

Agree on Guidelines: Establish guidelines and expectations for the use of technology, including response times and the types of information to be shared.

Focus on Transparency: Use technology to maintain transparency in all aspects of coparenting, including expenses, schedules, and communication.

Respect Privacy: Respect each other's privacy and only access or share information related to your child's well-being.

Stay Organized: Regularly update schedules and documentation to ensure that both parents are informed and organized.

Prioritize Child-Centricity: Always keep the child's best interests at the forefront of your communications and scheduling.

Professional Support: If using technology to communicate proves challenging, consider seeking professional mediation or therapeutic support to facilitate the process.

Leveraging Co-Parenting Apps and Tools for Effective Communication

In the realm of coparenting with a narcissistic ex-husband, co-parenting apps and tools can be a lifeline for effective communication, organization, and conflict resolution. Leveraging co-parenting apps and tools for effective communication can significantly improve your coparenting relationship, especially in high-conflict situations. These tools provide a structured and secure environment for managing schedules, documenting important information, and fostering a child-centric approach to co parenting. Here, we will delve into the strategies for making the most of these tools to enhance your coparenting relationship.

The Role of Co-Parenting Apps and Tools in Communication

Streamlined Communication: Co-parenting apps and tools offer a centralized platform for communication, reducing the need for face-to-face or direct interactions.

Documentation: These tools provide a means to document important information, including messages, schedules, and financial transactions, which can be crucial for clarity and evidence in case of disputes.

Transparency: Both parents have access to the same information, promoting transparency and accountability in the coparenting relationship.

Strategies for Effective Communication

Choose the Right Tool: Select a co-parenting app or tool that suits your specific needs and the level of cooperation between you and your ex-husband. Ensure both parents are comfortable with the platform.

Set Clear Communication Guidelines: Establish clear guidelines for communication, including response times, the types of information to be shared, and the use of notifications. Clear expectations help avoid misunderstandings.

Child-Centric Focus: Maintain a child-centric approach in all communication. The primary goal is to ensure the well-being and best interests of your child.

Use Neutral Language: Maintain a neutral and respectful tone in all written communication. Avoid emotional language or personal attacks.

Document Important Information: Utilize the tool's features to document important information, such as visitation schedules, school events, medical appointments, and expenses.

Keep Personal Matters Separate: Avoid discussing personal or emotional matters within the coparenting tool. These conversations are best held privately or in person.

Set Boundaries: Clearly define the boundaries of the coparenting tool. Use it exclusively for co parenting-related matters to prevent unrelated issues from complicating communication.

Regular Updates: Keep schedules and documentation up to date. Regularly check for new messages and updates to stay informed.

Resolve Disputes Through the Tool: When conflicts arise, use the coparenting tool to discuss and resolve them. This allows for documentation of the issue and any agreed-upon solutions.

Privacy and Security: Ensure that both parents are aware of and comfortable with the privacy and security features of the tool. Respect each other's privacy when using the platform.

Dealing with Resistance to Technology

If your ex-husband is resistant to using co-parenting apps or tools, consider the following strategies:

Highlight the Benefits: Emphasize the advantages of streamlined communication, organization, and transparency that these tools offer.

Demonstrate Ease of Use: Show your ex-husband how easy and user-friendly the tool is. Many co-parenting apps are designed to be intuitive.

Engage a Mediator: A neutral mediator can help facilitate discussions and guide both co parents in adopting co-parenting technology.

Legal Considerations: If court orders or custody agreements mandate the use of co-parenting tools, provide this information to your ex-husband to underscore the necessity of compliance.

Streamlining Schedules and Sharing Important Information

In the intricate landscape of coparenting with a narcissistic ex-husband, streamlining schedules and sharing vital information is essential for creating a structured and harmonious environment for your child. Efficient schedule management and information sharing are fundamental to successful co parenting, especially in high-conflict situations. By using technology and clear communication, you can provide a structured and stable environment for your child, minimize misunderstandings, and foster a supportive co parenting dynamic. Here, we will explore strategies for efficient schedule management and information sharing in your coparenting relationship.

Streamlining Schedules for Effective Co Parenting

Utilize Co-Parenting Apps: Leverage co-parenting apps or shared online calendars to maintain a synchronized and easily accessible schedule. These tools allow both co parents to view and update visitation dates, school events, extracurricular activities, and holidays.

Plan Well in Advance: Collaborate with your ex-husband to plan the schedule well in advance. This proactive approach can help prevent last-minute conflicts and provide stability for your child.

Include Important Details: Ensure that the schedule includes important details such as pick-up and drop-off locations, times, and any special instructions. Clarity and precision are crucial.

Flexibility: While maintaining a structured schedule is important, be prepared to accommodate reasonable changes or requests from your ex-husband. Flexibility can reduce conflicts and enhance cooperation.

Consistency: Strive for consistency in the schedule, particularly regarding routines and rules that both households should follow. A consistent environment can provide a sense of stability for your child.

Sharing Important Information in a Constructive Manner

Use Co-Parenting Apps: Co-parenting apps often provide dedicated sections for sharing information. Use these features to document and exchange essential details such as school reports, medical records, and visitation notes.

Be Transparent: Maintain transparency in sharing information. Make sure both parents have access to the same documentation and updates.

Prioritize the Child's Well-Being: Keep the child's best interests in mind when sharing information. Focus on matters directly related to their welfare.

Respect Privacy: While sharing information is essential, respect each other's privacy. Limit shared information to relevant child-related matters.

Use Neutral Language: Ensure that all communication and information sharing is conducted using neutral and respectful language. Avoid emotional or confrontational language.

Dealing with Resistance and Conflict

If you encounter resistance or conflict in streamlining schedules and sharing information:

Professional Mediation: Engage a professional mediator to facilitate discussions and provide guidance on effectively managing schedules and information sharing.

Legal Mandates: If court orders or custody agreements require shared information or the use of specific tools for co parenting, remind your ex-husband of these legal obligations.

Focus on the Child: Emphasize that efficient scheduling and information sharing ultimately benefit the child. Keeping the child's well-being at the center of discussions can motivate cooperation.

Privacy and Security: Ensure that both parents are comfortable with the privacy and security features of any co-parenting apps or tools being used. Address concerns related to privacy.
chapter 7

Real-Life Co-parenting Stories

In the world of coparenting, sharing real-life stories and experiences can provide valuable insights and inspiration. Real-life coparenting stories serve as a source of inspiration and guidance for those facing similar challenges. They demonstrate that, despite the difficulties and complexities of coparenting with a narcissistic ex-spouse, successful co-parenting is achievable through cooperation, communication, and a steadfast commitment to the well-being of the child. This chapter presents a collection of real-life coparenting stories, showcasing the challenges, successes, and lessons learned by individuals who have navigated the complexities of coparenting with a narcissistic ex-spouse.

Story 1: Finding Common Ground

In this story, a co-parenting couple initially faced intense conflict. However, they realized the negative impact it had on their child and decided to seek mediation. With the guidance of a skilled mediator, they learned to communicate more effectively and put their child's well-being first. Today, they successfully co parent by focusing on their child's happiness and adjusting their schedules to accommodate the child's needs.

Story 2: Embracing Technology

A mother and father in this story struggled with their ex-spouse's narcissistic behavior and consistent manipulation. They turned to co-parenting apps to streamline communication and reduce direct contact. These tools allowed them to maintain a structured schedule and share important information about their child without engaging in frequent conflicts.

Story 3: Rebuilding Trust

This story highlights a couple who initially had a tumultuous coparenting relationship due to lingering trust issues. They made the decision to seek therapy and counseling to address their emotional challenges. Over time, they rebuilt trust and learned to communicate more effectively. Today, they successfully co parent by emphasizing the importance of open and respectful communication.

Story 4: Navigating International Co Parenting

In this international co parenting story, a mother and father faced the additional challenge of living in different countries. They utilized online communication tools to bridge the geographical gap. While the distance presented challenges, they found creative solutions to maintain a strong connection with their child and adapt to the unique demands of international coparenting.

Story 5: Finding Support in Co Parenting Groups

A single mother faced severe challenges in coparenting with her narcissistic ex-husband. She joined a support group for co parents, where she found empathy, advice, and a strong sense of community. Through the group, she discovered effective coping strategies and leaned on the support of those who had faced similar difficulties.

Story 6: Prioritizing the Child's Needs

This story features a couple who recognized the detrimental impact of their high-conflict co parenting on their child's emotional well-being. They made a conscious decision to prioritize their child's needs, attend family therapy sessions, and implement a more cooperative co-parenting approach. The focus on the child's happiness became the driving force behind their successful co-parenting journey.

Learning from Others: Case Studies and Success Stories

In the realm of coparenting with a narcissistic ex-husband, drawing insights from real-life case studies and success stories can offer valuable lessons and inspiration. This chapter presents a collection of case studies and success stories, showcasing individuals who have navigated the complexities of coparenting with resilience and determination.

Case Study 1: Resilience in the Face of Tribulation

In this case study, a mother faced significant challenges coparenting with her narcissistic ex-husband. Through therapy and support groups, she developed coping strategies and learned to set firm boundaries. Over time, she successfully established a healthy co parenting dynamic focused on the well-being of her child.

This case highlights the power of resilience and the effectiveness of seeking professional and community support.

Case Study 2: Effective Communication in High-Conflict Situations

A father in this case study found himself in a high-conflict co parenting situation. By prioritizing effective communication and avoiding emotional triggers, he was able to navigate challenging interactions with his ex-wife. Through consistent efforts to maintain a child-centric focus, he successfully established a more cooperative coparenting relationship. This case emphasizes the importance of communication skills in managing high-conflict co parenting dynamics.

Case Study 3: Utilizing Technology for Streamlined Coparenting

In this case study, a couple faced difficulties in coordinating schedules and sharing information with their narcissistic ex-spouse. They turned to co-parenting apps to facilitate communication and organization. This shift enabled them to create a structured and efficient coparenting environment while minimizing direct conflict. This case highlights the practical benefits of leveraging technology in coparenting.

Case Study 4: Navigating International Co Parenting

A mother and father in this case study coparented across different countries, presenting unique challenges. They implemented a combination of video calls, shared online calendars, and email communication to maintain a strong connection with their child. Despite the distance, they successfully created a stable coparenting environment that prioritized the child's well-being. This case underscores the adaptability required in international co parenting situations.

Success Story 1: Finding Strength in Support Groups

A single mother faced the formidable task of coparenting with a narcissistic ex-husband. She joined a support group for co parents, which provided her with valuable advice, emotional support, and a sense of community. Through the group, she gained practical coping strategies and learned that she was not alone in her struggles. This success story highlights the transformative power of seeking support and finding strength in shared experiences.

Success Story 2: Prioritizing the Child's Well-Being

In this success story, a couple recognized the detrimental impact of their high-conflict co parenting on their child's emotional health. They committed to attending family therapy sessions, where they learned effective communication skills and conflict resolution techniques. By placing their child's well-being at the forefront, they successfully transitioned to a cooperative co-parenting approach. This success story illustrates the transformative potential of prioritizing the child's happiness.

Overcoming Challenges and Finding Solutions

In the realm of coparenting with a narcissistic ex-husband, facing challenges is inevitable. Let's delve into strategies for overcoming common challenges and finding practical solutions to maintain a healthy and child-focused coparenting relationship.

Challenge 1: High-Conflict Co Parenting

Solution: Mediation and Professional Support

If high conflict is a recurring issue, consider engaging a professional mediator or therapist to facilitate discussions and promote effective communication. Mediation sessions can provide a structured environment for conflict resolution, and therapists can help address underlying emotional challenges.

Challenge 2: Manipulation and Coercion

Solution: Establish Boundaries and Seek Legal Recourse

To address manipulation and coercion, it's crucial to establish clear boundaries in your coparenting relationship. If your ex-husband constantly violates these boundaries, consult with an attorney about potential legal recourse, such as restraining orders or modifications to existing court orders.

Challenge 3: Inconsistent Schedules and Communication

Solution: Co-Parenting Tools and Technology

Utilize co-parenting apps and tools to streamline schedules and maintain efficient communication. These platforms provide a centralized and organized environment for sharing information and coordinating visitation schedules.

Challenge 4: International or Long-Distance Co Parenting

Solution: Online Communication and Flexibility

In international or long-distance co-parenting situations, make use of online communication tools like video calls to stay connected with your child. Flexibility in visitation schedules is key, and it's essential to prioritize maintaining a strong bond despite geographical separation.

Challenge 5: Emotional Stress and Coping Difficulties

Solution: Seek Support and Self-Care

Managing emotional stress is vital. Seek support from professional therapists, support groups, or trusted family members or friends.

Prioritize self-care and stress management techniques, such as exercise, mindfulness, and relaxation practices, to maintain your emotional well-being.

Challenge 6: Legal Complexities

Solution: Consult with an Attorney and Document Violations

When faced with legal complexities, consult with an experienced family law attorney. Document any violations or disputes that may require legal intervention. An attorney can provide guidance and assistance in navigating the legal aspects of coparenting.

Challenge 7: Conflict Resolution

Solution: Effective Communication Skills

Develop effective communication skills, such as active listening, non-confrontational language, and conflict resolution techniques. Prioritize child-centric discussions and emphasize the best interests of your child in all interactions.

Challenge 8: Resistance to Co Parenting Tools

Solution: Highlight Benefits and Encourage Adoption
If your ex-husband is resistant to co-parenting tools, emphasize the benefits of streamlined communication and organization. Encourage their adoption by demonstrating the ease of use and their potential to reduce conflict.

Challenge 9: Financial Disputes

Solution: Transparent Expense Tracking and Mediation

Maintain transparent and detailed expense tracking to minimize financial disputes. In cases of persistent disagreements, consider mediation to resolve financial matters and ensure fair distribution of expenses.

Challenge 10: Safety Concerns

Solution: Legal Intervention and Documentation

For safety concerns, legal intervention may be necessary, including seeking restraining orders or modifications to court orders. Maintain thorough documentation of any instances or behaviors that raise safety concerns.

Setting Boundaries and Protecting Yourself

In the intricate landscape of coparenting with a narcissistic ex-husband, setting and maintaining clear boundaries is essential for preserving your emotional well-being and the stability of your coparenting relationship. Setting and maintaining boundaries is a fundamental aspect of managing a co-parenting relationship with a narcissistic ex-husband. It preserves your emotional well-being and the stability of the coparenting dynamic while ensuring that you can focus on the child's best interests. This chapter explores the importance of boundaries and strategies for protecting yourself in challenging co-parenting situations.

The Significance of Setting Boundaries

Emotional Protection: Boundaries shield you from the emotional turmoil that can arise in coparenting with a narcissistic ex-husband. They allow you to maintain your emotional equilibrium and focus on the child's well-being.

Conflict Reduction: Clear boundaries can minimize the potential for conflicts and confrontations by establishing expectations for respectful communication and behavior.

Preservation of Autonomy: Boundaries ensure that you maintain autonomy over your life, decisions, and personal space, even within the constraints of a coparenting relationship.

Strategies for Setting and Maintaining Boundaries

Define Clear Rules: Establish unambiguous rules and guidelines for communication, visitation, and interactions with your ex-husband. Ensure both parties understand and agree to these boundaries.

Maintain Written Records: Document any violations or issues that breach the established boundaries. These records can be valuable if legal intervention becomes necessary.

Seek Legal Recourse: If necessary, consult with an attorney to explore legal measures to enforce boundaries and protect your rights.

Prioritize Self-Care: Self-care is crucial for preserving your emotional well-being. Regularly engage in activities that bring you joy and relaxation, and make time for physical and mental health practices.

Seek Professional Support: Reach out to therapists, counselors, or support groups to help you develop effective strategies for setting boundaries and managing emotional challenges.

Avoid Engaging in Emotional Confrontations: Avoid getting drawn into emotional confrontations with your ex-husband. Instead, disengage and focus on addressing the issue calmly and rationally.

Supportive Co Parenting Tools: Leverage co-parenting apps and tools to facilitate communication while maintaining a controlled and structured environment for interaction.

Maintain Communication Etiquette: Use non-confrontational language and maintain a respectful tone in all communications with your ex-husband. Focus on the well-being of your child in your discussions.

Personal Support Network: Share your experiences and challenges with friends, family, or support groups. Their insights and advice can help you set and maintain boundaries effectively.

The Importance of Protecting Yourself

Safety: Prioritize your safety and that of your child. If you ever feel threatened or unsafe, seek legal protection and notify relevant authorities.

Emotional Well-Being: Protect your emotional well-being by managing stress, practicing self-care, and seeking professional support when needed.

Documentation: Maintain accurate records of interactions and conflicts to protect your interests and provide evidence if required in legal proceedings.

Autonomy: Safeguard your personal autonomy and decisions, ensuring that you maintain control over your life and choices.

Child's Best Interests: Protect your child's best interests by advocating for their welfare and stability, especially in situations where your ex-husband's behavior poses risks.

Addressing Safety Concerns and Seeking Help When Necessary

In the complex landscape of coparenting with a narcissistic ex-spouse, ensuring the safety and well-being of yourself and your child is paramount. Addressing safety concerns is a critical aspect of managing a co-parenting relationship with a narcissistic ex-spouse. Your well-being and the well-being of your child should be safeguarded above all else. Seeking help when necessary is a vital step in ensuring safety and maintaining emotional well-being in the coparenting dynamic.

Here, we will explore strategies for addressing safety concerns and seeking help when necessary in challenging co parenting situations.

Recognizing Safety Concerns

Emotional Abuse: Emotional abuse can manifest as manipulation, intimidation, or controlling behavior, which may create a hostile environment for you and your child.

Physical Safety: Safety concerns might extend to physical violence or the potential for harm, especially if there is a history of aggressive behavior.

Neglect: A narcissistic ex-spouse may neglect their parental responsibilities or disregard the child's well-being, which poses safety risks.

Mental Health Issues: Untreated mental health issues in your ex-spouse can also lead to safety concerns, particularly if they are unstable or unpredictable.

Strategies for Addressing Safety Concerns

Seek Legal Protection: If you have genuine safety concerns, consult with an attorney to explore legal options, such as restraining orders, supervised visitation, or modifications to custody agreements to protect yourself and your child.

Maintain Documentation: Document instances of safety concerns, including any incidents of emotional or physical abuse, neglect, or unpredictable behavior. This documentation can serve as evidence if legal intervention becomes necessary.

Safety Planning: Create a safety plan that outlines steps to take in case of emergency or escalating conflict. Share this plan with a trusted friend or family member.

Maintain Boundaries: Setting clear boundaries can help prevent unsafe situations and ensure that you and your child are protected from emotional or physical harm.

Seek Support: Reach out to a therapist or support group to help you cope with the emotional toll of safety concerns. Support can provide guidance on managing difficult situations and prioritizing your well-being.

Safety Concerns Involving the Child

Child Protection Services: In cases of severe neglect, abuse, or safety concerns related to your child, contacting child protection services may be necessary. This step should only be taken when the child's well-being is at risk.

Therapeutic Support for the Child: If your child is struggling with the emotional toll of safety concerns or difficult co parenting dynamics, consider seeking therapeutic support to help them navigate their feelings and experiences.

Court Intervention: In cases where child safety is a significant concern, consult with an attorney to address legal measures for ensuring the child's well-being, such as changes to custody arrangements or supervised visitation.

The Importance of Seeking Help

Safety First: Your safety and the safety of your child should always be the top priority. Seek help when you feel that your well-being or the child's well-being is at risk.

Emotional Support: Coparenting with a narcissistic ex-spouse can be emotionally challenging. Seek emotional support from professionals or support groups to help you manage these difficulties.

Legal Protection: If safety concerns persist, legal intervention may be necessary. Consult with an attorney to explore your legal options for protecting yourself and your child.

Thriving as a Coparent

Thriving as a co parent in the face of challenges, including coparenting with a narcissistic ex-spouse, is not only possible but also immensely rewarding. Thriving as a co parent involves embracing growth, prioritizing self-care, fostering supportive connections, nurturing your relationship with your child, and setting and achieving personal goals. By adopting a positive outlook and proactive approach, you can not only navigate the complexities of co parenting but also find fulfillment and growth in the process.

Here, we will explore strategies and mindset shifts that can help you not only navigate the complexities but also find fulfillment and growth in your co-parenting journey.

Cultivating a Growth Mindset

Embrace Change: Recognize that change is a natural part of life, and adapting to new circumstances is an opportunity for growth and learning.

Learn from Challenges: View challenges as opportunities for personal development and growth. Each obstacle presents a chance to develop resilience and problem-solving skills.

Focus on Solutions: Instead of dwelling on problems, shift your focus to finding constructive solutions. This proactive approach empowers you to take control of your co-parenting journey.

Prioritizing Self-Care and Well-Being

Physical Health: Regular exercise, balanced nutrition, and sufficient rest are foundational to maintaining your physical well-being.

Emotional Well-Being: Practice mindfulness, engage in activities that bring you joy, and seek support from professionals or support groups when needed.

Professional Growth: Continue to invest in your personal and professional development. Pursue opportunities for learning and growth in your career or personal interests.

Fostering a Supportive Network

Lean on Trusted Allies: Surround yourself with a network of trusted friends, family, or support groups who can offer guidance, understanding, and emotional support.

Seek Professional Guidance: Therapists, counselors, and legal professionals can provide valuable insights and guidance for managing co parenting challenges.

Join Co Parenting Groups: Engage in co parenting groups or communities where you can connect with others facing similar challenges. These forums offer a space for shared experiences and mutual support.

Nurturing Your Relationship with Your Child

Quality Time: Prioritize spending quality, one-on-one time with your child. Engage in activities they enjoy and create meaningful memories together.

Attentive Listening: Practice attentive listening to understand your child's aspective, feelings, and concerns. Validate their emotions and ensure a safe space for open conversation.

Consistency and Routine: Establish consistent routines and rules to provide stability and predictability for your child. This sense of structure can be trusted.

Setting and Achieving Personal Goals

Define Your Objectives: Clearly articulate your personal and professional goals. Whether they involve career advancement, personal hobbies, or self-improvement, having clear objectives provides direction.

Break Goals into Manageable Steps: Divide larger goals into smaller, actionable steps. This approach makes the process feel more attainable and allows you to track your progress.

Celebrate Progress: Acknowledge and observe your accomplishments, no matter how little. Recognizing your achievements fosters a sense of accomplishment and motivation.

Maintaining a Positive Outlook

Practice Gratitude: Cultivate a sense of gratitude for the positive aspects of your life, including the opportunities and experiences that arise from coparenting.

Focus on the Present: While it's important to plan for the future, staying present in the moment allows you to fully appreciate the experiences and connections in your life.

Visualize Success: Envision a thriving coparenting dynamic and the positive impact it has on your child's well-being. This visualization can serve as motivation during challenging times.

Empowering Yourself and Your Child for a Positive Future

In the realm of coparenting, empowering yourself and your child for a positive future is a transformative journey that ensures resilience, growth, and a hopeful outlook. Let us explore strategies and approaches to empower both you and your child, regardless of the challenges you may face.

Empowering Yourself

Self-Reflection: Engage in self-reflection to better understand your strengths, values, and goals. This self-awareness can guide your decisions and actions in the co-parenting journey.

Goal Setting: Set clear personal and professional goals that reflect your aspirations. These objectives will provide direction and motivation to move forward.

Resilience Building: Develop resilience by viewing challenges as opportunities for growth. Embrace setbacks as valuable experiences that ultimately lead to greater strength.

Self-Advocacy: Advocate for your needs and rights within the coparenting relationship. Clear and assertive communication can help you achieve your goals.

Seek Professional Support: If you encounter difficulties that seem insurmountable, consider seeking professional help. Therapists, counselors, and support groups offer guidance and emotional support.

Empowering Your Child

Encourage Independence: Support your child in gaining independence and making age-appropriate decisions. Empowering them to take control of their lives fosters self-confidence.

Educational Support: Invest in your child's education by providing resources, guidance, and encouragement to excel academically and explore their interests.

Emotional Resilience: Teach your child emotional resilience and coping strategies to navigate challenges and stressors. This skill set will serve them well in the future.

Self-Expression: Encourage your child's self-expression through art, writing, or any creative outlet they may find cathartic. Creative activities provide a safe space for emotional release.

Positive Role Modeling: Serve as a positive role model for your child by demonstrating the qualities and behaviors you hope to instill in them. Show them the importance of kindness, empathy, and self-care.

Planning for a Positive Future

Shared Goals: Collaborate with your child to set shared goals that align with their interests and values. This process fosters a sense of partnership and shared achievement.

Supporting Aspirations: Provide unwavering support for your child's dreams and aspirations, even if they may change over time. Your encouragement helps them build the confidence to pursue their goals.

Flexibility: Maintain flexibility in your co-parenting arrangement to accommodate your child's evolving needs and interests. Adapting to changes demonstrates your commitment to their future.

Higher Education and Career Planning: Offer guidance and resources for your child's higher education and career planning. Assist them explore various options and make informed decisions.

Building Strong Relationships: Foster healthy relationships within your child's life, including friendships, mentors, and other positive influences. These connections provide valuable support and encouragement.

Understanding your Child's Perspective

In the intricate journey of coparenting with a narcissistic ex-spouse, it's essential to always prioritize the child's well-being and understand their perspective. Minimizing the emotional impact on children is a fundamental aspect of creating a nurturing coparenting environment. By prioritizing their well-being, maintaining open communication, and providing a stable and consistent routine, you empower them to navigate co parenting challenges with resilience and strength. Here, we will delve into the importance of empathizing with your child's experiences, emotions, and needs during the coparenting process.

The Child's Coparenting Experience

Emotional Impact: Children in co-parenting situations often experience a wide range of emotions, including confusion, sadness, and anxiety. They may feel torn between their parents' conflicts.

Desire for Stability: Children typically crave stability and predictability. The coparenting environment should provide a sense of security and routine.

Sense of Belonging: Children desire a sense of belonging and connection with both parents. Ensuring that they maintain a bond with their narcissistic ex-spouse is vital.

Avoiding Conflict: Many children will go to great lengths to avoid witnessing or becoming involved in their parents' conflicts. Coparents should make efforts to minimize such exposure.

Strategies for Understanding the Child's Perspective

Open Communication: Create an environment in which your child feels comfortable expressing their thoughts and emotions. Encourage open dialogue and active listening.

Child-Centric Approach: Base all decisions and interactions on what is in the best interest of the child. Let this principle guide your coparenting dynamics.

Consistency and Predictability: Strive for consistency in routines and rules across both households to provide the child with a sense of stability.

Empathize with Their Emotions: Understand that your child may experience a range of emotions related to the divorce and coparenting. Show empathy and support their emotional well-being.

Minimize Conflict Exposure: Make every effort to shield your child from unnecessary exposure to conflicts between you and your ex-spouse. Avoid discussing adult issues in front of your child.

Maintain Both Relationships: Encourage and facilitate your child's relationship with their narcissistic ex-spouse. Be supportive of their need to maintain that connection.

Open Dialogue: Encourage open dialogue with your child about their feelings and concerns.

Ensure a safe space for them to communicate their feelings without judgment.

Therapeutic Support: If your child is struggling with the emotional toll of the divorce or coparenting, consider seeking therapeutic support to help them navigate their feelings and experiences.

Age-Appropriate Discussions: Tailor discussions and explanations to the child's age and level of understanding. Be honest but age-appropriate in your explanations

Minimizing Emotional Impact on Children

In the intricate dance of coparenting, minimizing the emotional impact on children is a crucial aspect of creating a stable, nurturing environment. This chapter delves into practical strategies and approaches to shield children from unnecessary emotional turmoil and help them thrive despite co parenting challenges.

Recognizing the Emotional Impact

Vulnerability of Children: Children are particularly vulnerable to the emotional dynamics of their parents' relationship. They may internalize conflicts or feel torn between their parents' feelings.

Long-term Effects: Unresolved emotional impact can have long-lasting effects on a child's emotional well-being, self-esteem, and overall development.

Importance of Co Parenting Stability: A stable, supportive co parenting environment helps mitigate the emotional impact on children and allows them to grow and flourish.

Strategies for Minimizing Emotional Impact

Child-Centric Decision-Making: Base all decisions related to co parenting on what is in the best interest of the child. Prioritize their needs and well-being.

Open Communication: Encourage open and age-appropriate communication with your child. Create a safe space for them to express their feelings and concerns without fear of judgment.

Avoid Exposing Them to Conflict: Shield your child from conflicts between co parents. Keep adult discussions separate from interactions with the child.

Maintain Consistency and Predictability: Establish consistent routines and rules in both households. Knowing what to expect provides a sense of stability for the child.

Reinforce Unconditional Love: Reiterate your love and support for your child. Make sure they understand that their worth is not tied to the dynamics between their parents.

Seek Professional Support: If you notice signs of emotional distress in your child, consider seeking the guidance of a therapist or counselor.

Professional support can help them navigate their feelings.

Empower Them with Age-Appropriate Information: Provide your child with honest, age-appropriate information about the co-parenting situation. This transparency helps them make sense of their experiences.

Encourage Coping Mechanisms: Teach your child healthy coping mechanisms for dealing with stress and emotions. This might include activities like journaling, art, or physical exercise.

Foster a Positive Co Parenting Environment: Lead by example in maintaining a positive, cooperative coparenting relationship. Show your child that healthy relationships are built on respect and communication.

Observing Signs of Emotional Distress

Changes in Behavior: Look for sudden shifts in behavior, such as withdrawal, aggression, or extreme mood swings.

Academic Decline: A noticeable decline in academic performance may be a sign that your child is struggling emotionally.

Regression: Younger children may exhibit signs of regression, such as bedwetting or reverting to behaviors they've outgrown.

Physical Symptoms: Pay attention to any unexplained physical symptoms like stomach aches or headaches, which can be indicative of emotional distress.

Isolation: If your child withdraws from social interactions or avoids activities they once enjoyed, it may be a sign that they're struggling emotionally.

Supporting Your Child's Emotional Well-Being

In the intricate world of coparenting, supporting your child's emotional well-being is a paramount priority. Supporting your child's emotional well-being is a foundational aspect of a nurturing coparenting environment. By actively listening, validating their emotions, and providing tools to manage stress and emotions, you empower them to navigate the challenges of coparenting with resilience and strength. Here, we will delve into practical strategies and approaches to create a nurturing environment that fosters emotional resilience and positive mental health in your child, despite the challenges of coparenting.

Prioritizing Emotional Well-Being

Understanding Emotional Needs: Recognize that your child has emotional needs, and it's crucial to prioritize and support their well-being.

Open Communication: Foster a relationship in which your child feels comfortable expressing their feelings and concerns. Encourage open and age-appropriate dialogue.

Emotional Resilience: Teach your child emotional resilience, which enables them to cope with stress, adversity, and emotional challenges effectively.

Practical Strategies for Supporting Emotional Well-Being

Active Listening: Listen actively and empathetically to your child. Show that their feelings are valid and important.

Validation: Validate your child's emotions, even if you don't share the same perspective. Let them know it's okay to feel the way they do.

Stress Management: Teach your child healthy stress management techniques, such as deep breathing, mindfulness, or physical exercise, to help them cope with challenging emotions.

Coping Mechanisms: Encourage your child to develop healthy coping mechanisms, such as journaling, art, or engaging in hobbies they enjoy.

Emotional Expression: Promote emotional expression through creative outlets like drawing, writing, or talking with a trusted adult. These activities provide a safe space for emotional release.

Positive Co Parenting Role Modeling: Demonstrate positive co parenting behavior. Show your child the importance of respectful communication, cooperation, and conflict resolution.

Addressing Specific Emotional Needs

Anxiety and Stress: If your child is experiencing anxiety or stress, provide them with tools and strategies to manage these emotions. Encourage relaxation techniques or seek professional support if needed.

Sadness or Grief: Address feelings of sadness or grief by acknowledging the child's emotions and providing a supportive, compassionate environment for them to process their feelings.

Anger: Teach your child constructive ways to express and manage their anger, such as communication, problem-solving, or physical activities that allow for release.

Fear or Uncertainty: Reassure your child by addressing their fears or uncertainties about the co-parenting situation. Provide age-appropriate explanations and offer support.

Self-Esteem and Self-Image: Foster a positive self-image in your child by consistently reinforcing their worth and helping them build self-esteem. Praise their accomplishments and qualities.

Professional Support and Therapeutic Guidance

Seek Professional Help: If you notice signs of emotional distress or if your child's struggles persist, consider seeking the guidance of a therapist or counselor. Professional support can help them navigate their feelings.

Therapeutic Tools: Therapists can provide therapeutic tools and strategies to help your child build emotional resilience and cope with challenges.

Support Groups: Explore support groups for children coping with similar emotional challenges. These groups provide a sense of belonging and shared experiences.

Conclusion

Navigating Coparenting with a Narcissistic Ex-Spouse. The journey of coparenting with a narcissistic ex-spouse is a formidable challenge, one that can test your emotional resilience, patience, and determination. Throughout this book, we've explored a myriad of strategies and approaches to not only navigate the complexities of co parenting but also to foster a nurturing, child-centric environment while safeguarding your well-being. This comprehensive guide aims to empower you with the knowledge and tools needed to thrive in the face of adversity.

The essence of successful co parenting lies in understanding the dynamics of narcissism and recognizing its impact on the relationship. By arming yourself with this knowledge, you gain the insight needed to navigate the manipulative behaviors and emotional challenges that often accompany narcissism. Recognizing these traits and setting boundaries are the initial steps towards building a healthier coparenting dynamic.

Coping with a narcissistic ex-spouse requires emotional fortitude and resilience. Strategies for maintaining your emotional well-being, such as self-care, support networks, and positive thinking, play a pivotal role in helping you withstand the emotional challenges that may arise. Seeking therapy or support groups can provide invaluable guidance and a safe space to share your experiences and concerns.

One of the cornerstones of effective co parenting is putting your child first. A child-centric approach prioritizes their emotional well-being, stability, and a nurturing environment. It involves open communication, consistency, and minimizing conflict exposure to ensure that your child thrives despite the challenges of coparenting.

Addressing safety concerns is an essential aspect of this journey. When necessary, seeking legal protection and maintaining documentation can help ensure your safety and the safety of your child. Empowering yourself, seeking help when needed, and focusing on solutions are crucial to managing difficult situations.

Threading through the challenges of coparenting, you can thrive as a co parent. Cultivating a growth mindset, prioritizing self-care, nurturing a supportive network, and setting and achieving personal goals empower you to not only survive but also to flourish in the face of adversity.

Empowering yourself and your child for a positive future is the culmination of this journey. By instilling independence, emotional resilience, and self-expression in your child, you equip them to face the future with confidence and strength. Collaborating on shared goals and offering unwavering support, you can plan for a future full of opportunities and success, regardless of the challenges you may encounter in coparenting.

I've A Request

Dear Reader,

I hope you've found the information and insights in this book valuable and informative. Your feedback is incredibly important in helping us improve and create even better resources in the future. If you could spare a few moments to share your thoughts by leaving a review, we would greatly appreciate it. Your review will not only assist us in refining our content but also guide other readers who may be seeking assistance and guidance.

Thank you for taking the time to read our book and for considering leaving a review. Your input is truly invaluable.

Warm regards,

Sara C. Blackmon